S0-AGB-585

3 9082 11003 8044

ALLEN PARK PUBLIC LIBRARY
8100 ALLEN RD.
ALLEN PARK, MI 48101
2425

ALLEN PARK PUBLIC LIBRARY
8100 ALLEN RD.
ALLEN PARK, MI 48101

DISCARD

J332.4C

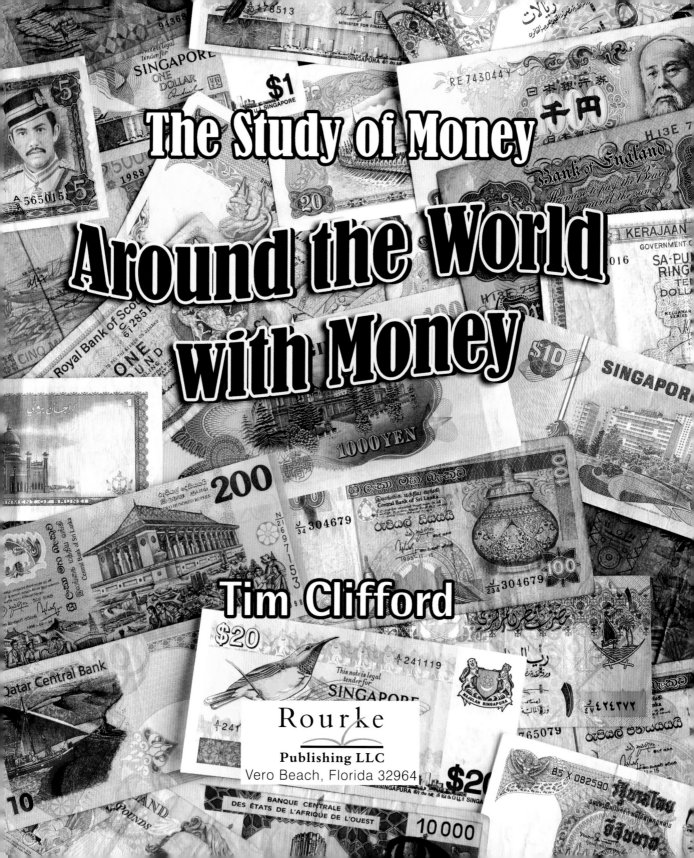

The Study of Money

Around the World with Money

Tim Clifford

Rourke

Publishing LLC

Vero Beach, Florida 32964

© 2009 Rourke Publishing LLC

All rights reserved. No part of this book may be reproduced or used in any form or by any means, electronic or mechanical, including photocopying, recording, or by any information storage and retrieval system without permission in writing from the publisher.

www.rourkepublishing.com

PHOTO CREDITS: © Joel Blit: page 4 top; © Timothy E. Goodwin: page 4 bottom; © Christopher David Howells: page 5; © Kaspars Grinvalds: page 6 top; © Samuel Kessler: page 6 bottom; © Illustrious: page 7, 11, 17, 19, 21; © Les Byerly: page 8 top; © Doug Coldwell: page 8 bottom; © Jon Gorr: page 9 right; © Grafissimo: page 9 left; © Angelo Gilardelli: page 10; © Philip Lange: page 12; © Andre Maritz: page 14 top; © Albo: page 14 bottom; © Jean Schweitzer: page 15 top left; © Zoran Djekic: page 15 top right; © TTphoto: page 15 bottom right; © Daniel Gustavsson: page 15 bottom left; © Tyler Olson: page 16; © Helios: page 18; © Sean O. S. Barley: page 20; © Mityukhin Oleg Petrovich: page 22 top right, Peru 25, Venezuela 25, 27 top, 29; © Siddligatta Viswakumar: page 22 top left; © Agb: page 23 top; © Vinicius Tupinamba: page 24; © Akva: Chile page 25; © Themalau: page 26 bottom; © Jonathan Noden-Wilkinson: page 27 bottom; © Jan Hopgood: page 28; © Christophe Testi: page 30

Editor: Jeanne Sturm

Cover Design: Renee Brady

Page Design: Tara Raymo

Library of Congress Cataloging-in-Publication Data

Clifford, Tim, 1959-
  Around the world with money / Tim Clifford.
      p. cm. -- (The study of money)
  Includes index.
  ISBN 978-1-60472-403-5
  1. Money--Juvenile literature. I. Title.
  HG221.5.C56 2009
  332.4--dc22

                                    2008011330

Printed in the USA

IG/IG

3 9082 11068 8044

Table of Contents

World Currencies

If you want to learn about a country, look at its money, or **currency**. Most countries make their own money. Money can reflect the language, **culture**, and even some of the history of the country that makes it.

You can find flags and pictures of important people on a country's currency. You may also find a **motto**, or a phrase, that tells you something about the beliefs of that country. All American coins bear the motto E Pluribus Unum (Latin for From Many, One).

Each currency has its own standard unit of value. For example, the United States uses the dollar as its standard unit. Each unit comes in different **denominations**, or values. The smallest U.S. denomination is one penny (1/100th of a dollar) and the largest is one hundred dollars.

Each currency has its own ISO 4217 code. This three letter code is used by businesses and money **exchanges**. The first two letters stand for the country's name. The third letter represents the name of its currency. The ISO 4217 code for the Japanese yen is JPY. The JP stands for Japan, and the Y for yen, Japan's currency.

Most countries also use a currency symbol, such as $, for the U.S. dollar.

The United States Dollar

The U.S. dollar is the official currency of the United States. It was introduced in 1785, less than a decade after the United States declared its independence from England.

The dollar, like many other world currencies, is divided into hundredths. One cent is equal to one hundredth of a dollar. Nine countries besides the United States use the dollar as their currency. Because of its popularity, many other countries also accept the U.S. dollar as payment.

Facts about U.S. Currency

Basic Unit	The Dollar
ISO 4217 Code	USD
Currency Symbol	$ (dollar), ¢ (cent)
Pictured on the Dollar	George Washington, the first president of the United States
Coins	1¢, 5¢, 10¢, 25¢, 50¢, $1
Paper Money	$1, $2, $5, $10, $20, $50, $100
Interesting Fact	One nickname for the dollar is the greenback. It got the name from the color on the reverse of the bill.

7

Many people think the mint produces all United States currency, but actually the U.S. Mint produces only coins. Paper money is printed by the Bureau of Engraving and Printing.

To keep up with demand, more than 750 million dollars worth of paper money is printed every day. Most of it is used to replace paper money already in **circulation**.

United States currency has a lot in common with other types of money throughout the world. For example, U.S. currency is stamped with its denomination. It honors great citizens by putting their **portraits** on the **obverse**, or front. All U.S. currency contains the words *In God We Trust.*

9

The Euro

Prior to 1999, most European countries had their own currencies. Since then, fifteen of those countries have joined together to create a single currency called the euro. Countries that use the euro include Austria, Belgium, Cyprus, Finland, France, Germany, Greece, Ireland, Italy, Luxembourg, Malta, the Netherlands, Portugal, Slovenia, and Spain. Several other smaller nations use the euro unofficially.

Like the U.S. dollar, the euro is divided into 100 cents. They are called eurocents.

Facts about the Euro

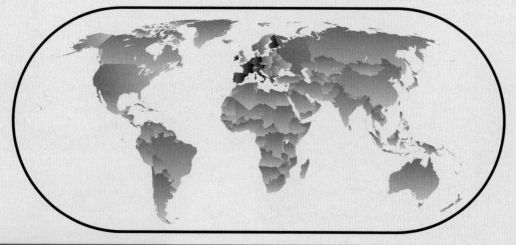

Basic Unit	The Euro
ISO 4217 Code	EUR
Currency Symbol	€
Pictured on the One Euro Coin	A map of the European Union (EU)
Coins	1, 2, 5, 10, 20, and 50 eurocents, €1, €2
Paper Money	€5, €10, €20, €50, €100, €200, €500
Interesting Fact	In 2006, the total value of euros worldwide was greater than the total value of U.S. dollars for the first time.

11

While the **reverse**, or back, of every euro is the same, the obverse, or front, is different. Each country that issues a coin is allowed to put its own **design** on the front. A coin issued by one country is accepted by all other countries that use the euro.

The designs on paper euros are the same for all countries.

Countries in the European Union that have adopted the euro as their official currency are part of the Eurozone. Over 350 million people live in the Eurozone and use the euro as their currency.

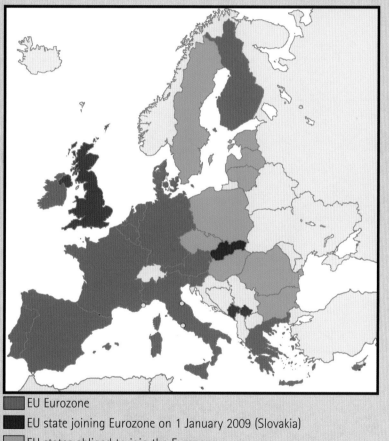

- EU Eurozone
- EU state joining Eurozone on 1 January 2009 (Slovakia)
- EU states obliged to join the Eurozone
- EU state with an opt-out on Eurozone participation (U.K.)
- EU state planning to hold a referendum on the euro and with an opt-out on Eurozone participation (Denmark)
- Areas outside the EU using the euro with an agreement
- Areas outside the EU using the euro without an agreement

13

Other European Money

While most European nations have adopted the euro, a few have not. The United Kingdom, Denmark, and Sweden still use their own currency.

The United Kingdom

A pound in the United Kingdom doesn't refer to weight. The pound is the name for the official currency of the UK. The symbol for the pound is £ and the code is GBP. The pound is divided into 100 pence (or pennies).

Denmark

The official currency of Denmark is the krone. In English, the word krone means crown. The symbol for the krone is kr and the code is DKK.

Sweden

The currency of Sweden is also called a crown, or krona. Like the Danish krone, the symbol is kr, but the code is SEK.

15

Canadian Money

    Just as in the United States, Canada uses the term dollar for its currency. It uses the same symbol, $. To make it clear which is being talked about, the symbol C$ is often used to refer to Canadian money. It is also divided into 100 cents.

    While most U.S. dollars are paper, the Canadian dollar is a coin. Because a picture of a loon is stamped on the coin, it is often referred to as a loonie.

Facts about Canadian Currency

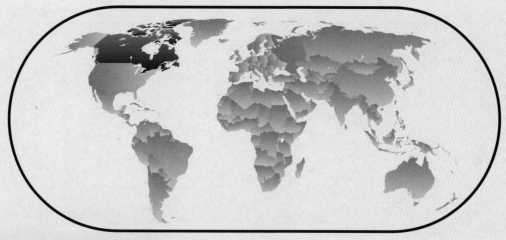

Basic Unit	The Dollar
ISO 4217 Code	CAD
Currency Symbol	$ (dollar), ¢ (cent)
Pictured on the Front	The Canadian Loon
Coins	1¢, 5¢, 10¢, 25¢, 50¢, $1, $2
Paper Money	$5, $10, $20, $50, $100
Interesting Fact	The two dollar Canadian coin is nicknamed the toonie after the one dollar loonie.

17

Mexican Money

In the 19th century, the Spanish dollar was used in much of the United States and Mexico. Later, the peso became the official currency of Mexico. It was about the same size and weight as the Spanish dollar. The peso is divided into 100 centavos.

While Mexico mints many different coins, only a few are common in circulation. The 1000 peso note is an unusually large denomination.

Facts about Mexican Currency

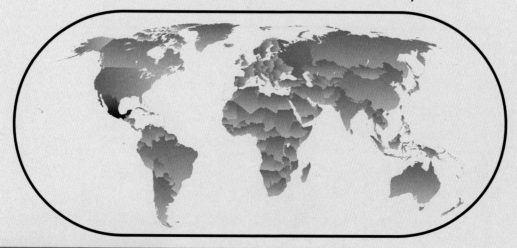

Basic Unit	The Peso
ISO 4217 Code	MXN
Currency Symbol	$ (peso), ¢ (centavo)
Pictured on the Peso	The symbol $1
Coins	20¢, 50¢, $1, $2, $5, $10, $20
Paper Money	$20, $50, $100, $200, $500, $1000
Interesting Fact	A new peso was introduced in 1993. One new peso is equal to 1000 older pesos.

Japanese Money

The Japanese yen is the third most traded currency in the world, after the United States dollar and the euro. The yen is both the basic unit and the smallest denomination of Japanese money in use.

The pictures on Japanese paper money are quite interesting. They include a scientist and two authors.

Facts about Japanese Currency

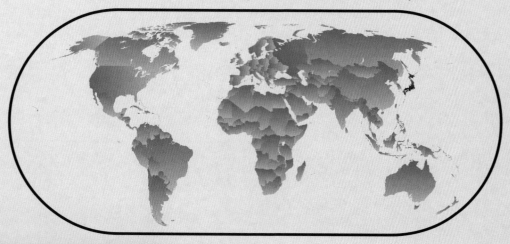

Basic Unit	The Yen
ISO 4217 Code	JPY
Currency Symbol	¥
Pictured on the Yen	A tree with branches growing upward
Coins	¥ 1, ¥ 5, ¥ 10, ¥ 50, ¥ 100, ¥ 500
Paper Money	¥ 1000, ¥ 2000, ¥ 5000, ¥ 10000
Interesting Fact	The word yen means circle. Early yen were circular with a square or round hole in them.

Money in Asia

Many countries in Asia besides China and Japan have their own currencies. Let's look at the money from some of the larger Asian nations.

India

All circulating coins in India are adorned with the emblem of India. All of its paper money bears the portrait of Mahatma Gandhi, one of India's greatest leaders. The code for the Indian rupee is INR, and its symbol is Rs.

South Korea

The basic unit of South Korean currency is the won. Like the Chinese word yuan and the Japanese word yen, won means circle. Pictured on the won is the Hibiscus syriacus, which is the national flower of South Korea. The code for the won is KRW, and its symbol is ₩.

Russia

The ruble is an ancient currency. The first rubles were made over five centuries ago. Today, the ruble is still the official currency of Russia. A two headed eagle is stamped on the one ruble coin. The code for the ruble is RUB. It has no official symbol.

Saudi Arabia

The riyal is the official currency of Saudi Arabia. It is divided into hundredths called halalahs. Most current paper money shows the portrait of Saudi Arabia's King Abdullah. The code for the riyal is SAR, and its symbol is SR.

Money in South America

Brazil

The largest country in South America is Brazil. Its currency is the real. It is divided into 100 centavos. The real comes in both a coin and a paper money version. The code for the real is BRL, and its symbol is R$.

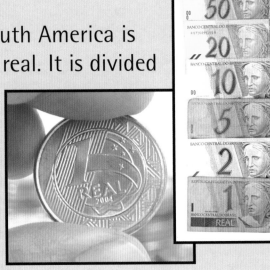

Argentina

Second in size to Brazil is Argentina. Its official currency is the peso. Like the Brazilian real, the peso is divided into 100 centavos. The peso coin shows a picture of a sun. The two and five peso coins honor two famous Argentineans, author Jorge Luis Borges and first lady Eva Perón. The code for the peso is ARS, and the symbol is $.

Many other countries in South America issue their own currency.

Bolivia

Boliviano

Chile

Chilean Peso

Columbia

Columbian Peso

Guyana

Guyanese Dollar

Paraguay

Guarani

Peru

Nuevo Sol

Suriname

Surinamese Dollar

Uruguay

Uruguayan Peso

Venezuela

Bolivar

Ecuador uses the U.S. dollar as its currency. French Guyana uses the euro.

Money in Africa

There are far too many countries in Africa to list all their currencies here. Some interesting currencies are discussed below.

Algerian Dinar (DZD)

The word dinar comes from the denarius, which is one of the oldest coins of ancient Rome.

Congolese Franc (CDF)

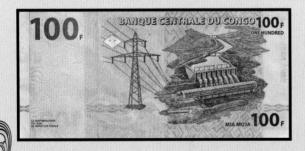

The Democratic Republic of the Congo used to be known as Zaire. It was once ruled by Belgium, which also used the franc.

Kenyan Shilling (KES)

Kenya has a very strong currency, so some other African nations use it as well. The paper money is very colorful and striking.

South African Rand (ZAR)

Rand banknotes come in many colors and depict animals native to Africa, such as the lion and rhinoceros.

27

Money in Australia

The **continent** of Africa contains many countries, but Australia is a continent and a single country in one. Because of this, the Australian dollar is the currency across the entire continent. The Australian dollar, like the U.S. dollar, is divided into 100 cents.

Paper money in Australia is unique because it isn't paper at all. It is made of polymer, a plastic. These notes last longer and they are hard to **counterfeit**. Australian dollars are among the most colorful in the world.

Facts about Australian Currency

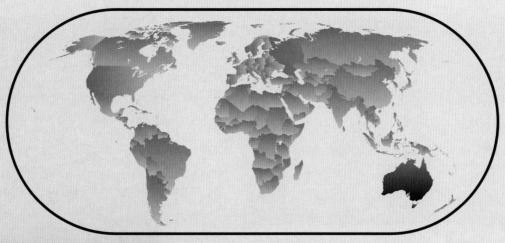

Basic Unit	The Dollar
ISO 4217 Code	AUD
Currency Symbol	$ (dollar), c (cent)
Pictured on the Dollar	Queen Elizabeth II
Coins	5c, 10c, 20c, 50c, $1, $2
Paper Money (Polymer)	$5, $10, $20, $50, $100
Interesting Fact	There is no Australian one cent coin.

Currency Exchanges

Most airports have a currency exchange.

All currencies are not equal. This is especially true when it comes to the value of different currencies. One United States dollar does not buy the same amount of goods as one Chinese yuan, for example.

Because of this, you must exchange your currency before you travel. If you go to Europe, you will need euros. If you go to Mexico, you will need pesos. To get them, you go to a currency exchange.

There, you can change your money into whatever currency you need.

Glossary

circulation (sur-kyuh-LAY-shun): the amount of bills and coins in use

continent (KON-tuh-nuhnt): one of the several large land masses of the Earth, including Asia, Africa, Europe, North America, South America, Australia, and Antarctica

counterfeit (KOUN-tur-fit): something that has been made to look like the real thing but is fake, such as counterfeit money

culture (KUHL-chur): the way of life, ideas, customs, and traditions of a people

currency (KUR-uhn-see): the form of money used in a country

denominations (di-nom-uh-NAY-shuhnz): values or units in a system of measurement

design (di-ZINE): an outline, sketch, or plan

exchanges (eks-CHAYNJ-iz): places where people give one kind of currency and receive another type

motto (MOT-oh): a short sentence that is meant to guide behavior or state what someone believes or stands for

obverse (OB-vurss): the front of a coin or bill

portraits (POR-trits): drawings, paintings, or photographs of a person

reverse (ri-VURSS): the back of a coin or bill

Index

Further Reading

Giesecke, Ernestine. *From Seashells to Smart Cards: Money and Currency.* Heinemann, 2003.

Kummer, Patricia. *Currency.* Franklin Watts, 2005.

Websites

www.finance.yahoo.com/currency?u

www.fx.sauder.ubc.ca/currencies.html

www.banknotes.com/images.htm

About the Author

Tim Clifford is an educational writer and the author of many nonfiction children's books. He has two wonderful daughters and two energetic Border Collies that he adopted from a shelter. Tim became a vegetarian because of his love for animals. He is also a computer nut and a sports fanatic. He lives and works in New York City as a public school teacher.